COLLECTION
and
PRESERVATION
of
INSECTS

U. S. DEPARTMENT OF AGRICULTURE

Fredonia Books
Amsterdam, The Netherlands

Collection and Preservation of Insects

by
P. W. Oman
Arthur D. Cushman

for U.S. Department of Agriculture

ISBN: 1-4101-0858-9

Reprinted from the 1958 edition

Fredonia Books
Amsterdam, The Netherlands
http://www.fredoniabooks.com

INSECTS are of many kinds and differ greatly in their life histories and habits. From the viewpoint of man, some insects are injurious, some are unimportant, and some are beneficial. Because of these differences it is important to recognize insects, in order that our war against injurious species may be carried on effectively.

Well-preserved and properly labeled specimens are essential to the identification of insects. This publication gives information on collecting, preserving, handling, mounting, and labeling insect specimens, on subsequent care of collections, and on recognition of the general insect groups, or orders. It has been prepared in response to numerous requests from farmers, students, servicemen, and other individuals and groups interested in obtaining first-hand knowledge of insects by collecting them.

COLLECTION AND PRESERVATION OF INSECTS

By P. W. OMAN, *senior entomologist,* and ARTHUR D. CUSHMAN, *chief scientific illustrator, Agricultural Research Service*

Contents

Page

What to collect _____ 2
Equipment and collecting methods
  Nets _____ 2
  Killing bottles _____ 5
  Aspirator, or suction bottle_____ 7
  Beating cloth, or umbrella_____ 8
  Sifters _____ 9
  Separators _____ 9
  Collecting at lights_____ 9
  Baits and bait traps_____ 10
  Tweezers, forceps, and brushes___ 10
Rearing _____ 11
How to kill and preserve specimens 12
Care and handling of unmounted
  specimens _____ 14
How to mount insects_____ 14
  Direct pinning _____ 15
  Double mounts _____ 18
  Inflation of larvae _____ 19
  Riker mounts _____ 20
  Spreading boards and blocks____ 20
  Relaxing jars _____ 22
Labeling the specimens_____ 22
  What information is essential____ 22
  How to make labels _____ 23
  How labels should be pinned____ 24
Care of the collection _____ 24
  Housing _____ 24

Page

Protection from pests _____ 24
Packing and shipping specimens____ 25
  Live insects _____ 25
  Dead insects _____ 25
  Packing for shipment_____ 25
Recognition of material _____ 25
  Thysanura _____ 28
  Collembola _____ 28
  Orthoptera and Dermaptera_____ 28
  Isoptera_____ 29
  Plecoptera _____ 29
  Ephemeroptera _____ 31
  Odonata_____ 32
  Corrodentia _____ 32
  Mallophaga _____ 32
  Anoplura _____ 32
  Thysanoptera _____ 33
  Hemiptera _____ 33
  Coleoptera _____ 35
  Neuroptera _____ 37
  Zoraptera _____ 37
  Megaloptera _____ 37
  Mecoptera _____ 38
  Trichoptera _____ 38
  Lepidoptera _____ 39
  Diptera _____ 40
  Siphonaptera _____ 41
  Hymenoptera _____ 42

WE ARE constantly at war with insects. Year after year insects are responsible for enormous losses in terms of disease and destruction of food, clothing, and other materials of value to man. In order to combat insects successfully we must know them well; we must know where they live, what they feed upon, and how they develop.

The habits of one kind of insect may be very different from those of another very similar in appearance. For this reason we cannot generalize, but must obtain definite information about each species. The better we know our insect enemies, the better are our chances of anticipating attacks and of preparing and conducting our defenses against them.

We have to be ever on the alert for new pests and new outbreaks of old pests, and to do this we must be able to distinguish between insects that are injurious or potentially injurious and those that are beneficial or of no consequence to human welfare. Increasing knowledge of the damage done by insects, and especially recent discoveries concerning the role they play in the transmission of animal and plant diseases, emphasize anew the necessity for correctly identifying these pests. Otherwise we dissipate our efforts and misuse our ammunition, so to speak, in the destruction of beneficial or unimportant insects.

Because the correct identification of insects is seldom easy, it is important that specimens be preserved in as good condition as possible. The identification of a particular species of insect usually requires examination of minute details of its anatomy with the aid of a lens or a microscope. If these details are concealed or missing because of improper handling and preservation, then it is impossible to identify the specimens, and previously existing information about the habits, economic importance, and control of the species cannot be found and utilized.

This bulletin has been prepared to fill the needs of farmers and other persons and groups interested in the study and control of insects. It is also intended for use in meeting the numerous requests received from those who desire information on methods of collecting and preserving insects. Furthermore, it should be helpful to agencies engaged in conducting insect surveys as a basis for pest control.

It will give needed guidance in the collection of different kinds of insects and in the preservation of such material in a manner that will permit definite identification. The instructions given are necessarily brief. Additional information may be obtained by writing to the Entomology Research Division, Agricultural Research Service, United States Department of Agriculture, Washington 25, D. C.

WHAT TO COLLECT

What to collect will depend on the purpose for which the material is intended. Insects which are important as pests and for which identification is needed should always be collected in numbers. A sample of 20 specimens should be the minimum, and even more are desirable. It is a good rule always to collect an adequate sample of all the different stages, regardless of whether the insect is observed to be a pest. Specimens can always be discarded or exchanged, but it is not always possible to collect additional specimens at the time they may be needed for study.

Most persons will find it desirable to concentrate on one or two of the major insect groups. There are so many insects—more than 80,000 kinds are known in North America alone—that it is scarcely possible for one person to assemble a collection that includes examples of all those occurring in a single locality.

The collection of specimens alone is not enough. Information about them is equally important. The collector should take advantage of opportunities to observe and record interesting facts about the habits and life histories of the different insects found, for in this way he may add important details to the growing store of knowledge that enables us successfully to compete with our insect enemies.

EQUIPMENT AND COLLECTING METHODS

The equipment required for assembling a representative insect collection need not be elaborate or expensive. Most needs of the average collector will be met by the items discussed in the following pages.

Much equipment for collecting insects may be purchased from commercial supply companies, most of which will send catalogs and price lists on request. Below are given the names and addresses of a few such companies. The United States Department of Agriculture does not guarantee or endorse the firms listed or the reliability of their products. In furnishing this list no claim is made that it is complete.

Central Scientific Company, 1700 Irving Park Road, Chicago, Ill.
Clay-Adams Company, Inc., 141 East 25th Street, New York, N. Y.
E. H. Sargent and Company, 4647 West Foster Avenue, Chicago 30, Ill.
General Biological Supply House, 8200 South Hoyne Street, Chicago 20, Ill.
Southern Biological Supply Co., 517 Decatur Street, New Orleans 16, La.
Standard Scientific Supply Corp., 34–38 West Fourth Street, New York 12, N. Y.
Supply Department, Marine Biological Laboratory, Woods Hole, Mass.
Ward's Natural Science Establishment, 3000 Ridge Road, Rochester 9, N. Y.

NETS

Construction

Although a considerable variety of nets may be purchased from supply houses, many collectors prefer to make their own. The insect net consists essentially of a cloth bag hung from a metal loop attached to a handle. Figure 1, which shows parts of a beating, or sweeping, net, illustrates the general principles involved in the construction of

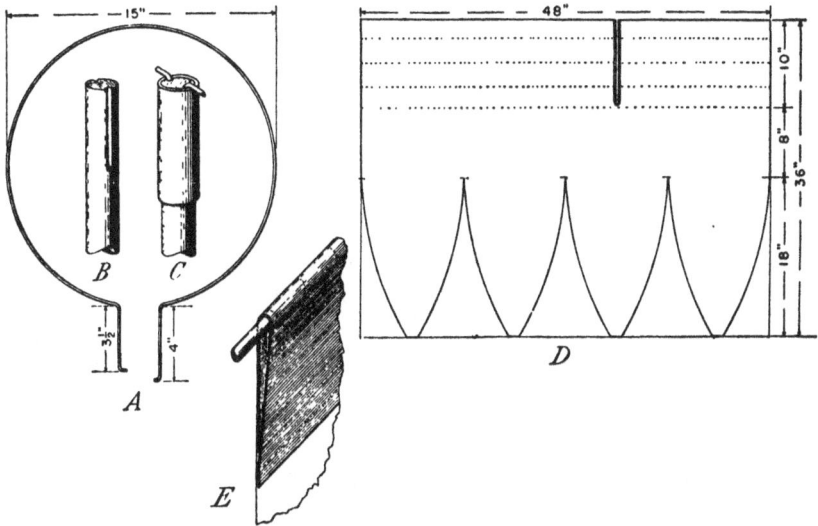

FIGURE 1.—The construction of a beating net: *A*, Steel wire loop 15 inches in
diameter; *B*, end of net handle showing grooves and holes into which the arms
of the wire loop fit; *C*, net handle with metal ferrule to hold net in place;
D, how to cut a single piece of cloth to make a round-bottom bag; *E*, details of
top part of net fitted over a section of the wire loop.

the insect net, but the size and shape of the net and the material used
will depend upon the purpose for which it is intended.

The beating net must be strong enough to stand rough use. A handle
of straight-grain hickory or ash, such as a hoe handle, is recommended.
This should be fitted at one end with a metal ferrule (fig. 1, *C*) about
an inch in diameter to hold the wire loop in place. The grooves in
the handle should be made exactly as long as the straight arms of the
net loop, so that the tips of the arms, bent at right angles, will fit into
the holes bored in the handle at the end of the grooves. The rest of
the handle should be about 1⅜ inches in diameter and 3½ to 4½ feet
long.

The wire loop (fig. 1, *A*) should be of steel wire which will spring
back in shape if bent. For the beating net No. 12 steel wire (0.189
inch in diameter) is satisfactory, although even heavier wire is sometimes preferred. After the loop is shaped it is usually desirable to
have it tempered and, if this can be done at a factory or shop where
steel springs are made, a most satisfactory net loop will result.

For the bag for the beating net, 6-ounce drill, heavy muslin, or
light canvas is recommended. Figure 1, *D*, illustrates how a bag to
fit a loop 15 inches in diameter may be made from a single piece of
material. The four lobes, cut as segments of a circle, form the rounded
bottom of the bag when sewed together. The slit at the top, which
should be cut and hemmed as indicated before the top of the bag is
folded over, permits the completed bag to be slipped onto the wire
loop. The top margin of the material should then be folded down
to the bottom dotted line and sewed in place; then this double thick-

ness of material should be stitched through in a zigzag fashion and turned down again to form the wide hem by means of which the bag is attached to the wire loop. The details of this double-thickness hem as it hangs on the wire loop are shown in figure 1, *E*. Because that part of the bag gets the most wear it is usually advisable to make it of the double thickness of material indicated. The zigzag stitching keeps the outer thickness from fraying so badly when it wears through. If desired, a single thickness in the top band of the bag may be later reinforced by some heavy material, or, in the case of a light-weight bag, the entire top band may be made of a stout material and the light-weight bag sewed to this. The final step is to complete the bag by sewing together the two ends of the material and the margins of the cut lobes. The completed bag may be slipped onto the wire loop by squeezing the loop together and sliding the net band on a little at a time.

The beating net described above is not satisfactory for the capture of moths, butterflies, flies, wasps, and other swift-flying or fragile insects. For collecting these the nets described in the next three paragraphs will be found useful.

The general-purpose net should have a loop 12 inches in diameter and a bag of unbleached muslin or coarse- or medium-mesh brussels. This net should be tapered more toward the bottom than the beating net but should not come to a point. The handle need not be as stout as that for the beating net.

The butterfly net is like the general-purpose net, but the bag is of good-quality marquisette or fine netting and the handle is a little longer and of lighter weight. This net is also useful in capturing dragonflies and other large-winged insects.

The fly net should have a loop 8 inches in diameter and a bag of medium-mesh brussels or fine netting. The handle should be short and light. The wire loop need not be so heavy as that for the beating net. This net is also good for collecting bees and wasps.

The aquatic net, for collecting insects that live in or on water or on aquatic plants, should not have a circular loop but should be either square, with the handle attached to one corner, or about semicircular, with the side opposite the handle straight. The bag should be shallow (about as deep as the length of the straight side in the semicircular net) and should be made of heavy scrim with a canvas band for the wire loop.

The bag for any of the nets described above may be made of silk bolting cloth, which is very durable and comes with meshes of various sizes. However, bolting cloth is expensive and difficult to obtain and is not recommended for the general collector. The bag for any net, excepting the water net, should be long enough so that the tip may be flipped over the rim of the wire loop to form a pocket from which the netted insects will not escape.

Care and Use

Nets should be kept dry. A wet net damages the specimens and dampness causes the fabric to rot quickly. Aquatic nets should be thoroughly dried after use.

Although the beating net may be used on thorny bushes and trees, most other nets tear easily and should be used with care. Insects should be removed from the beating net after a few sweeps so that they will not be battered by the debris that accumulates in the net. Lively insects, such as leafhoppers, can be easily removed from the beating net with an aspirator. (See p. 7.) To do this, stand so that the open end of the net is not directly toward the sun, rest the loop of the net on your head, and, if possible, let the bag of the net be distended by the wind. Thus one hand is free to manipulate the bag and the other to handle the aspirator, while the head and arm of the collector fill the opening of the net sufficiently to prevent the escape of most specimens.

In using the fly net or butterfly net, after the captured specimen has been enclosed in the tip of the net by grasping the bag with one hand a little from the end, insert the open killing bottle into the net and permit the specimen to drop into it. While the bottle is still in the net, cover the opening until the specimen becomes stupefied; otherwise it may escape before the bottle can be removed from the net and closed.

KILLING BOTTLES

Construction

Any fairly heavy glass jar or vial with a wide mouth is satisfactory for a killing bottle, and every collector should have several bottles of various sizes. Empty pickle jars, olive jars, and the like will furnish a considerable assortment of larger bottles, and smaller ones may be made from test tubes or shell vials 1 to 1½ inches in diameter. These should be supplied with tight-fitting corks or screw caps. A and B of figure 2 illustrate two bottles of convenient shape. Figure 2, C, illustrates a convenient adaptation of a screw cap for a jar to keep bees, grasshoppers, and other lively insects from escaping from the killing bottle when it is opened for putting in other specimens. This cap is made by soldering an incomplete metal cone to a screw cap with the top cut out. A metal tube ¾ to 1 inch in diameter is then soldered inside the cone.

Chemicals

Various chemicals may be used in the bottles for killing agents; two of the best are discussed below.

Cyanide.—Calcium cyanide, potassium cyanide, or sodium cyanide may be used. Wrap some granular cyanide (a heaping teaspoonful for small bottles, larger amounts for large bottles) in cellucotton, or place it in a "nest" in cellucotton or a little cloth bag, and put this in the bottom of the bottle. Over this place a plug or several layers of cellucotton or a layer of dry sawdust. Cellucotton is inexpensive and may be purchased at most large drug stores or from supply houses. If the bottle is more than 1½ inches in diameter, a ¼-inch layer of plaster of paris should be poured in and allowed to harden for a few hours before the bottle is corked. If the bottle is a small one, several disks of clean blotting paper, cut to fit the bottle snugly, may be used in place of the plaster of paris.

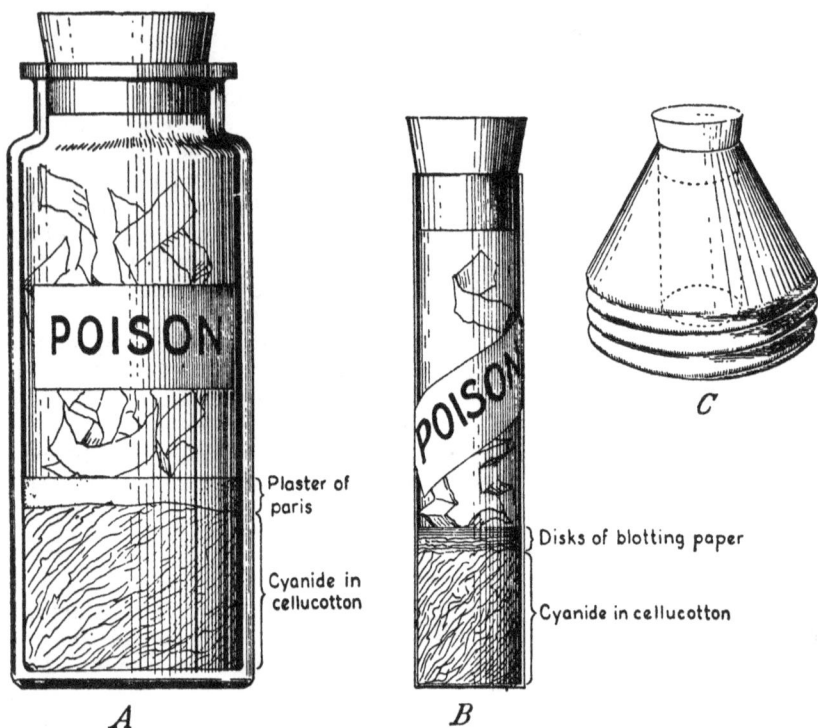

FIGURE 2.—Killing bottles: *A*, Large, wide-mouth cyanide bottle for large insects; *B*, vial-type cyanide bottle for small insects; *C*, screw-cap top for large cyanide bottle, showing a convenient arrangement to prevent the escape of active specimens.

Cyanide is a deadly poison and should be handled with great care. All bottles should be conspicuously labeled "POISON" and should be kept away from people who do not realize the deadliness of the chemical. The bottom of a cyanide bottle should be taped so that if the bottle is broken the cyanide will not be scattered about.

Ethyl acetate.—To make a killing bottle in which to use ethyl acetate (acetic ether), pour a half inch or more of plaster of paris into the bottom of a suitable jar or vial, allow it to set, and dry it thoroughly in an oven. After the plaster of paris is completely dry, saturate it with ethyl acetate, pouring off any excess fluid. The killing bottle is then ready for use and will last for months if kept tightly corked. When it becomes ineffective it can be dried in the oven and recharged. Insects may be preserved in such bottles for an indefinite time without becoming brittle, provided they receive an occasional moistening with ethyl acetate. Ethyl acetate is relatively easy to obtain, and the killing bottles have the obvious advantage of being comparatively safe to use.

The killing bottle will last longer and give better results if the following simple rules are observed:

1. Before using the cyanide bottle, put in a few strips of soft paper. Ordinary toilet paper is excellent. This will help keep the bottle dry and will keep the specimens from mutilating one another. Change these strips whenever they become soiled or slightly moist. Wipe out the bottle if it becomes moist.

2. Keep a special bottle for moths and butterflies. The scales from these insects will stick to other insects and spoil them.

3. Never put small or delicate insects in the same bottle with large insects such as grasshoppers and large beetles. Beetles are hard to kill and must be left in the killing bottle longer than most other insects.

4. Never overload a bottle, and always remove insects from the cyanide bottle as soon as they are dead.

5. Discard or recharge bottles that no longer kill quickly. Dispose of the contents of old cyanide bottles by burning or burying.

Many insects should not be killed in a killing bottle but should be placed in 70-percent alcohol or some other fluid. These insects are discussed in more detail later in this bulletin. For these insects the collector should have a supply of small homeopathic vials of various sizes with corks to fit.

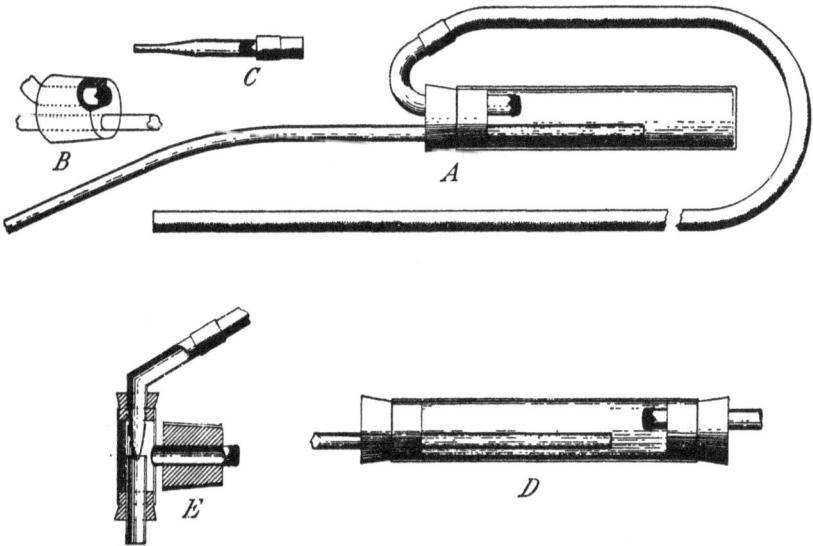

FIGURE 3.—Aspirator, or suction bottle: *A*, Vial-type aspirator assembled; *B*, details of stopper assemblage for vial-type aspirator, showing outlet tube flush with surface of stopper; *C*, attachment for collecting tiny insects with an ordinary aspirator; *D*, body of tube-type aspirator; *E*, details of construction to convert an aspirator to the blow type.

ASPIRATOR, OR SUCTION BOTTLE

The aspirator is a convenient device for collecting small insects, either from the beating net or beating cloth or directly from under stones, bark, etc. Its construction is rather simple and needs little discussion. For the type illustrated in figure 3, *A*, the following materials are needed:

1. A glass vial 1 to 1½ inches in diameter and about 4½ inches long.
2. A rubber stopper with two holes in it.
3. Two pieces of metal or plastic tubing, one about ¼ inch in diameter and 10 inches long, the other slightly larger and 4 or 5 inches long.
4. A piece of rubber tubing about 3 feet long and big enough to slip onto the larger of the metal or plastic tubes.
5. A small piece of bolting cloth or fine-mesh wire screen.

The metal tubes should fit snugly in the holes in the rubber stopper. The shorter metal tube should be bent as indicated so that the rubber tubing will not fold shut when in use. The bolting cloth should be fastened over the end of the larger metal tube as shown; this is to keep the insects from being sucked into the mouth. If wire screen is used it may be soldered to the end of the metal tube. It is desirable, but not necessary, to have the shorter tube come flush with the end of the cork, as in figure 3, *B*. If metal or plastic tubing is not available or cannot conveniently be bent to suit, glass tubing may be used but has the disadvantage of breaking easily. The length and size of the tubing, as well as the degree of the bends, may be adapted to the user's convenience.

When the aspirator is assembled, place the end of the rubber tubing in the mouth, aim the longer tube of the aspirator at a small insect, and suck sharply. The air current will pull the insect into the vial. With a little practice it is possible to collect small insects much more quickly and in better condition this way than by almost any other method.

A convenient attachment for collecting thrips, very small flies, beetles, and other insects normally killed in liquid is illustrated in figure 3, *C*. By means of a short section of rubber tubing a tapered piece of glass tubing 2 or 3 inches long is attached to the intake tube of the ordinary aspirator. A piece of fine-mesh bolting cloth, inserted in the glass tubing near the large end, keeps the tiny insects from going on into the aspirator. They can then be blown out into the vial of liquid in which they are to be preserved. This attachment is easily put on and taken off, and having it makes it unnecessary to carry a small aspirator.

Some collectors prefer the tube-type aspirator, the body of which is illustrated in figure 3, *D*. Either the tube-type or the vial-type aspirator may be converted to a blow-type collecting bottle by substituting for the shorter tube, to which the rubber tubing is attached, the attachment illustrated in figure 3, *E*. This piece of equipment makes use of an air current to create a partial vacuum, and with it in use in the assembled aspirator, the same result is obtained by blowing instead of sucking through the rubber tubing. This type of attachment is essential if the aspirator is to be used to collect insects that emit noxious odors.

BEATING CLOTH, OR UMBRELLA

Instead of beating vegetation with a net, it is sometimes convenient to have a cloth surface over which shrubby plants can be beaten. For this purpose the beating cloth, or umbrella, is suggested.

The beating cloth should be about 1 yard square, of durable material, and preferably white. It may be stretched nearly flat by fastening the corners to a frame made by crossing and fastening together two pieces of light wood, one of which should project a little beyond the corner of the cloth to serve as a handle. The umbrella is used inverted and should have the handle jointed so that the umbrella may easily be held upside down below branches and bushes. When in use, both the beating cloth and the umbrella are held below the vegetation while the branches are struck sharply with a club. In this way many insects will be jarred onto the cloth and can be readily captured. These pieces of equipment are also handy when pulling bark from trees and, when so used, will catch many specimens that would otherwise escape.

SIFTERS

Many insects spend all or part of their lives in ground litter and leafmold. These cannot be captured by ordinary collecting methods, and because they are too active to be caught by hand, or they feign death when disturbed, a sifter should be used.

Almost any container with a wire-mesh bottom will serve as a sifter. The size of the meshes in the screen will depend upon the size of the insects sought; for general purposes a screen with eight meshes to the inch will be satisfactory. The screen may be fastened to a wooden frame to make a box-shaped sifter, or it may be attached to a wire hoop, which is then sewed to one end of a cloth sleeve about 12 inches in diameter. In the latter type of sifter it is convenient to have a wire hoop of the same size at the other end of the cloth sleeve to hold it open.

Place the leafmold or ground litter in the sifter and shake it gently over a piece of white oilcloth spread flat on the ground. As the insects fall onto the cloth they may be easily captured with an aspirator or tweezers. Many insects feign death and are not easily seen until they move, so the debris on the cloth should not be discarded too quickly. The sifter is especially useful for winter collecting.

SEPARATORS

The collector who wishes to obtain large numbers of the small insects that are usually found in ground litter will find it advantageous to construct a separator (usually called a Berlese funnel by entomologists) for use instead of the sifter. Fundamentally, the separator consists of a funnel over which a sieve containing leafmold or other litter may be placed. The funnel leads into a receptacle containing a liquid preservative, into which the insects fall when driven from the material in the sieve by the progressive drying with a light bulb or some other source of mild heat. Many separators, some very elaborate, have been devised by entomologists, but all rely on the same basic principles. Details of construction may be obtained by writing to some entomological institution.

COLLECTING AT LIGHTS

Collecting at lights, especially on warm, humid nights, frequently permits the collector to obtain in abundance insects that are captured rarely or not at all by other methods. While light traps, many types of which have been devised, are of use to entomologists for making surveys to determine the abundance of certain insects in restricted regions, their use as a means of obtaining insects for the collection is not recommended because the specimens are too frequently damaged. Insects for the collection should be selected and captured by attending the light continuously while it is in operation.

Although any reasonably bright light will serve, more insects are attracted to blue lights than to other kinds. A convenient method of collecting at a light is to hang up a white sheet so that the light shines upon it, turn up the lower edge to form a trough into which some of the insects will fall, and collect the specimens as they come to the sheet. Many insects may also be collected around street lights and lighted store windows.

BAITS AND BAIT TRAPS

Baits of many kinds are valuable aids to the collector. One of the best known uses for baits is in "sugaring" for moths. For sugaring, make a mixture of molasses or brown sugar, a little asafoetida, and stale beer, rum, or fermenting fruit juices, and daub it on tree trunks along a route that can be conveniently visited with a lantern or flashlight. As with light collecting, this method is most productive on warm, humid nights. The bait should be applied about dusk and may be visited at intervals all that night and frequently will be found to be attractive to insects on succeeding nights. Moths, ants, and many other insects will be found at the bait.

Insects that are attracted to either sweet substances or decaying meat may be captured in simple jar traps. Bait the jar (an olive bottle or a fruit jar will do) with an appropriate bait, and bury it with the open top flush with the surface of the ground. It is frequently desirable to set these traps under loose boards or stones lying on the ground.

TWEEZERS, FORCEPS, AND BRUSHES

The collector will find it advantageous to have available an assortment of tweezers and brushes as an aid both in collecting and in handling the specimens after they are dead. Equipment of this kind may be purchased at small cost from most biological supply houses.

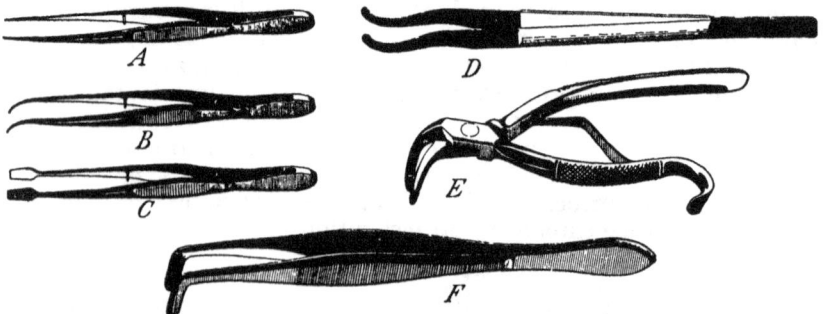

FIGURE 4.—Tweezers and forceps: A and B, Types of tweezers for handling ordinary specimens; C, tweezers for handling unmounted Lepidoptera; D, tweezers for handling living, soft-bodied insects; E and F, two types of pinning forceps.

Three standard types of tweezers are illustrated in figure 4, *A*, *B*, and *C*. Tweezers of the straight-pointed type are ideal for bending the tips of card points on which to mount small specimens and will be useful for many other purposes. However, some workers prefer the curved tips for handling specimens. The tweezers shown in figure 4, *C*, are best for handling dead butterflies, as the tips will not break through the wings so readily as will the points of the tweezers shown in *A* and *B*. Figure 4, *D*, illustrates a pair of tweezers that may be made from two pieces of flexible steel spring. These are ideal for handling living or dead specimens with very soft bodies.

A few small camel's-hair brushes, sizes 0 to 2, are handy for picking up small insects that might be crushed if handled with tweezers. Moisten the tip of the brush on the tongue or in the liquid preservative, touch the specimen with the brush, and you can transfer it safely to the collecting vial. If brushes are not available, the moistened end of an ordinary flat toothpick is a satisfactory substitute.

Figure 4, *E*, illustrates a type of dental forceps that is recommended as a pinning forceps. The curved tips permit the pin to be grasped below the pin labels, and thus even very slender pins can be set firmly into cork without bending.

REARING

Whenever possible, the collector should avail himself of the opportunity to rear insects, for by so doing he may secure many insects otherwise obtained only rarely. In addition, the specimens will frequently be in much better condition than collected material, and there is an opportunity to make valuable observations on the biology of the species reared. If abundant material is available for rearing, it is always advisable to preserve a few specimens of each of the various stages according to instructions given later in this bulletin, so that the complete life history of the species will be represented. If only a few specimens are being reared, the shed skins of the specimens should be preserved, as these are of value also.

To rear specimens successfully the natural conditions under which the immature insects were found should be simulated as closely as possible in the rearing cages. Insects that feed on living plants may be caged over potted plants or fed frequently with fresh material from their host plant. With a little ingenuity a suitable cage can be prepared; the important thing is to have it tight enough to keep the insects in and yet provide for sufficient ventilation so that the container will not "sweat." Some loose, slightly moist soil and ground litter should be provided in case the insect is one that pupates in or on the ground. Insects that feed on decaying animal matter should also have the cage provided with slightly moist soil or sand.

Insects that infest seeds and those that cause plant galls may be reared merely by enclosing the seeds or galls in a tight container. Such material should not be permitted to become too dry; neither should it be kept moist, else the material and the specimens will mold. It is a good plan to insert the open end of a glass vial through a hole in the container; then, if the container is dark, when the specimens emerge they will be attracted to the light, enter the vial, and can be easily removed and killed. Tiny parasitic wasps may be reared from their hosts in this manner. A cardboard ice-cream container is excellent for this type of rearing.

Adult moths, butterflies, beetles, and many other insects may be obtained by collecting pupae and caging them until the specimens emerge. In this way the best specimens of moths and butterflies may be secured. Always permit the reared specimen to harden and color completely before killing it, but do not leave it in the cage so long that it will damage itself in trying to escape. Cages should always be placed where they will be safe from ants.

Very often bark and wood infested by boring insects, such as beetles, are found. If these are placed in glass or metal containers, excellent specimens of the adults may be obtained. Cages of wood and cardboard should be avoided for obvious reasons. Such material can often be collected and caged during the winter months, the period of effective field collecting being thus extended.

HOW TO KILL AND PRESERVE SPECIMENS

The method of killing and preserving to be used depends upon the kind of insects involved. No one method is satisfactory for all specimens, and it is necessary for the collector to have some knowledge of what is being collected in order properly to care for the material. Frequently it is desirable to kill in liquid any specimens that will later be pinned for the collection. The best general liquid killing and preserving agent, which should always be used unless some other preservative is especially recommended, is 70- to 75-percent grain (ethyl) alcohol. Formalin, which is frequently used as a preservative for biological specimens, is not recommended as a preservative for insects because it hardens the tissues and makes the specimens difficult to prepare for study. In the discussion that follows, alcohol, unless otherwise indicated, means 70- to 75-percent grain alcohol.

The procedure to be followed for all insects killed in alcohol but later mounted dry is as follows:

1. Kill in alcohol.
2. Dehydrate in 100-percent alcohol (200 proof, also called absolute alcohol). This step takes from 1 to 24 hours, depending on the size of the specimens.
3. Degrease in xylene (zylol) or benzene (benzol). This step requires about the same length of time as the dehydration. If specimens retain a milky film in the xylene they have not been completely dehydrated.
4. Remove from xylene, dry, and mount.

Specimens killed in the ethyl acetate killing bottle, but which contain considerable fatty tissue (lipoids), should be degreased before being mounted. Any of a number of lipoid solvents may be used, the most satisfactory of which is ordinary commercial sulfuric ether. Soak the specimens in the ether bath until the fluid ceases to become yellow from the dissolved oils, changing the fluid if necessary. The length of time necessary for complete degreasing will vary from a day to a week, depending upon the size and number of specimens, their fat content, and the volume of ether used. A wad of absorbent tissue or filter paper should be placed in the bottom of the container to absorb waste that accumulates and which might otherwise cling to the specimens.

Ether has the disadvantage of being highly inflammable and must be used with great care. Other solvents which may be used are chloroform, benzene, xylene, and diethyl carbonate. If chloroform is used, the specimens must be held submerged by a wire screen. After being degreased, specimens should be transferred to a clean pad of absorbent tissue and their appendages arranged; after they are sufficiently dry they may be mounted.

Specimens that contain but little fatty tissue (lipoids), and hence do not ordinarily become greasy, may be killed in the cyanide jar or the ethyl acetate killing bottle and mounted without further preparation. Pinned specimens that have become greasy owing to the decomposition of body fats may be degreased by being put in an ether or chloroform bath for a few hours. Other killing agents, such as carbon tetrachloride, ether, chloroform, and benzene may be used, but each has some objectionable features, and they are not recommended for general use.

Some insects, such as scale insects, aphids, lice, thrips, and other minute forms, can be satisfactorily studied only after they are mounted on a microscope slide. These insects should be killed and preserved according to the instructions which follow, but the proper preparation of slide mounts is a task requiring considerable equipment and experience, and slide preparations should not be attempted without the aid of specific instructions, which are usually different for different groups of insects.

The following outline gives instructions for killing and preserving the commoner types of insects and also indicates the usual method of mounting for study. Methods of mounting specimens on pins are discussed in detail later in this bulletin. The steps between killing and mounting specimens killed in alcohol or the ethyl acetate killing jar have been outlined above and are not repeated here. Descriptions and illustrations of common representatives of most of these insect groups are given under Recognition of Material, page 26.

Anoplura (sucking lice) : Kill and preserve in alcohol; mount on slides.
Coleoptera (beetles) : Kill in alcohol or ethyl acetate vapor; mount on pins.
Collembola (springtails) : Kill and preserve in alcohol; mount on slides.
Corrodentia (booklice) : Kill and preserve in alcohol.
Dermaptera (earwigs) : Kill in cyanide, ethyl acetate vapor, or alcohol; mount on pins.
Diptera (flies) : Kill in cyanide, except minute forms, such as eye gnats and fungus gnats, which should be killed in alcohol; mount on pins.
Ephemeroptera (Mayflies) : Kill and preserve in alcohol.
Hemiptera (true bugs and their allies) : Kill in cyanide, ethyl acetate vapor, or alcohol, except the immature stages, aphids, scale insects, and Aleyrodidae (whiteflies) ; mount on pins. Nymphs should be killed in alcohol and mounted on pins. Aphids should be killed in alcohol and mounted on slides. Scale insects and whiteflies on host material should be preserved dry, but if they are not on host material they should be preserved in alcohol; mount on slides.
Hymenoptera (bees, wasps, ants, etc.) : Kill in cyanide, except ants, gall wasps, and small parasitic forms, which should be killed in alcohol; mount on pins.
Isoptera (termites) : Kill and preserve in alcohol.
Lepidoptera (moths and butterflies) : Kill in cyanide; mount on pins.
Mallophaga (biting lice) : Kill in alcohol; mount on slides.

Mecoptera (scorpion flies) : Kill in cyanide; mount on pins.
Neuroptera (lacewing flies, ant lions, etc.) : Kill in cyanide; mount on pins.
Odonata (dragonflies) : Kill in cyanide; mount on pins.
Orthoptera (grasshoppers, crickets, roaches) : Kill in cyanide; mount on pins.
Plecoptera (stoneflies) : Kill and preserve in alcohol.
Siphonaptera (fleas) : Kill in alcohol; mount on slides.
Thysanoptera (thrips) : Kill in a liquid made of 8 parts 95-percent alcohol, 5 parts distilled water, 1 part glycerin, and 1 part glacial acetic acid; mount on slides.
Thysanura (silverfish and their allies) : Kill and preserve in alcohol.
Trichoptera (caddisflies) : Kill in cyanide; mount on pins.
Zoraptera : Kill and preserve in alcohol.
Larvae of insects should be killed in boiling water and allowed to remain in the water from 1 to 5 minutes, according to size, then preserved in alcohol.
Centipedes, millipedes, mites, spiders, ticks, and other small arthropods, although they are not insects, are frequently handled by entomologists. All these should be killed and preserved in alcohol. The smaller forms are usually mounted on slides.

CARE AND HANDLING OF UNMOUNTED SPECIMENS

It is frequently impracticable to mount all collected specimens soon after they are killed, and some method of caring for them so they will not be broken must be used. Specimens collected in liquid may be preserved in the liquid indefinitely without injury, the only precaution being to keep plenty of fluid in the container. Specimens that are killed in the ethyl acetate bottle and are intended for the ether bath may also be preserved indefinitely in a container with just enough ethyl acetate to keep them from drying.

Specimens that are killed in cyanide and are to be mounted without further treatment will soon become dry and brittle. Such material should be placed in paper pill boxes between layers of cellucotton cut to fit the box and packed tightly enough so that the specimens will not shift about, but not pressed down enough to flatten or distort the specimens. The pill box should be filled with layers of cellucotton, even though all the layers are not needed for specimens. Cotton should not be used, as legs and antennae catch on the fibers and are apt to be broken off. Medium-sized and small Lepidoptera should be packed one specimen to a layer of cellucotton. Large Lepidoptera, Odonata, and other insects with large wings and relatively small bodies should be placed in envelopes or folded "triangles," which may then be packed between layers of cellucotton. The method of folding a rectangular piece of paper to form a "triangle" is shown in figure 5. The specimen should be placed in the folded triangle in the position shown in figure 5, B.

When storing unmounted specimens, do not forget to write the collection data on the pill box or on the end of the envelope or "triangle."

HOW TO MOUNT INSECTS

Specimens are mounted to facilitate handling and study, and their value increases with the convenience with which they may be examined and compared with specimens of the same or related species. As a result of years of experience by many workers there have been

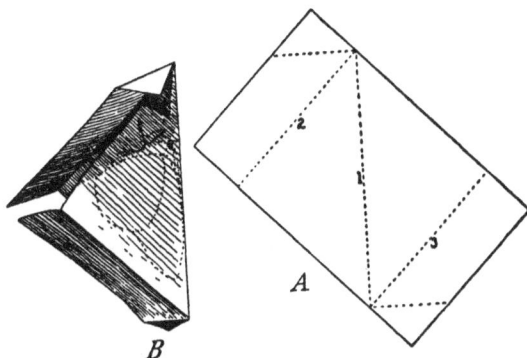

FIGURE 5.—Method of folding a rectangular piece of paper to form a triangular envelope for large-winged insects: *A*, Correct shape of unfolded paper, showing where the folds should be made and the sequence of the first three folds; *B*, "triangle" almost completely folded, showing correct position of the enclosed butterfly.

developed standard pinning practices, designed to avoid injury to the specimens and to expedite study. Although methods of preparing specimens are constantly being improved, currently accepted practices should be observed in the interest of uniformity until the superiority of other methods has been clearly demonstrated.

DIRECT PINNING

Ordinary household pins are too short and thick and should not be used for pinning insects. Insect pins, which may be purchased from supply houses, should be of good-quality spring steel and thoroughly japanned so as to be nearly rustproof. They may be obtained in numbered sizes and different lengths suitable for pinning insects of various sizes. For most purposes No. 2 or No. 3 pins 34 mm. long will be found satisfactory, although a smaller size, No. 1, may occasionally be desirable for small flies, and larger and longer pins, such as No. 4 or No. 5 pins 37 or 39 mm. long, are better for large-bodied moths, beetles, and cicadas. A comparison of a millimeter scale with the more familiar inch scale is given in figure 6.

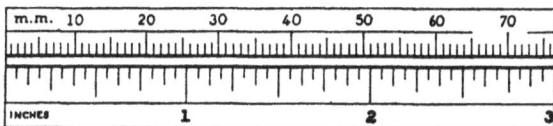

FIGURE 6.—Comparison of inch and millimeter scales. A centimeter equals 10 millimeters.

Medium-sized and large insects should be pinned vertically through the body with a pin of appropriate size. Figures 7 and 8 illustrate some right and wrong pinning practices. Before pinning a specimen it is well to examine the under side so as to be sure that the pin will not break off a leg where it comes through. The standard methods for pinning the commoner types of insects are as follows:

1. Grasshoppers, katydids, etc.: Pin through the back part of the thorax to the right of the middle line (fig. 9, A).

2. Stinkbugs and other large Hemiptera: Pin through the scutellum to the right of the middle line (fig. 9, C).

3. Bees, wasps, and flies: Pin through the thorax between or a little behind the bases of the forewings and to the right of the middle line (fig. 9, D).

4. Beetles: Pin through the right wing cover near the base (fig. 9, E).

5. Moths, butterflies, dragonflies, and damselflies: Pin through the middle line of the thorax at the thickest point or between or a little behind the bases of the forewings (fig. 9, F, G).

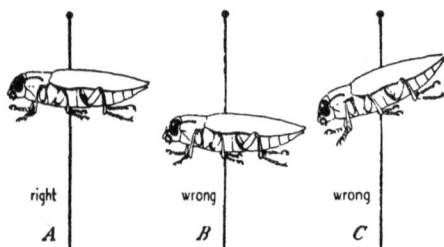

FIGURE 7.—Illustration of right and wrong methods of pinning: A, Correct height and position for specimen; B, insect too low on the pin; C, insect tilted on the pin.

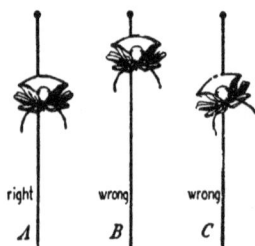

FIGURE 8.—Illustration of right and wrong methods of pinning: A, Correct height and position for specimen; B, insect too high on the pin; C, insect tilted on the pin.

The height of the specimen on the pin will depend somewhat on the size of the specimen. In general, there should be enough room at the top of the pin so that it may be handled without the fingers touching the specimen. With a little practice this may be judged accurately; if uniformity is desired, the specimen may be adjusted to the desired height on the pin by using the pinning block shown in figure 10.

After being pinned, and before being permitted to dry (or after being thoroughly relaxed if already dried), the legs, wings, and antennae of the specimen should be properly arranged so they are visible for study. The correct arrangement of legs and antennae for grasshoppers and related forms is shown in figure 9, B. With many insects, such as beetles, bugs, flies, and bees, it is only necessary to arrange the legs and antennae and they will stay in place. With grasshoppers, however, it is usually necessary to pin the specimens close to the edge of a box so that other pins to hold the legs in place may be thrust into the sides of the box at various angles. With some specimens, such as wasps and long-legged flies and bugs, the legs and abdomen may be kept in place until dry by pushing a piece of stiff paper up on the pin beneath them.

Moths, butterflies, and sometimes grasshoppers, dragonflies, and cicadas, should have the wings on one or both sides spread. For this purpose a spreading board is necessary. The construction and use of the spreading board is discussed on page 19.

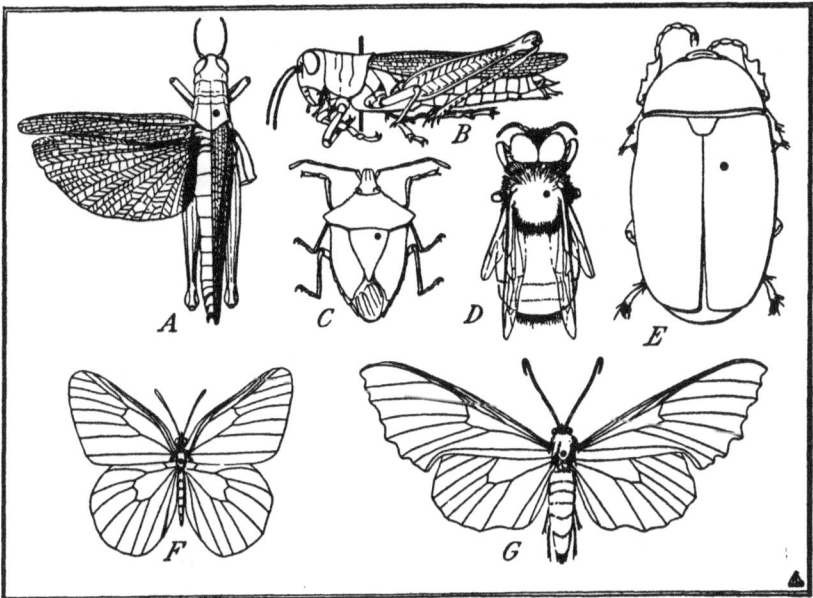

FIGURE 9.—Examples of correct pinning methods for common insects; the black spots show where the pins should go. A, Grasshopper and related Orthoptera, showing how wings should be spread; B, side view of a grasshopper, showing position of legs and antennae; C, a stinkbug, an example of the order Hemiptera, showing method of pinning large bugs; D, a bee, order Hymenoptera, to show where bees, wasps, and flies should be pinned; E, a May beetle, order Coleoptera, showing method of pinning beetles; F, G, butterfly and moth, order Lepidoptera, showing location of pin and position of wings and antennae.

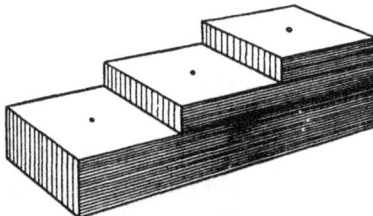

FIGURE 10.—Pinning block for adjusting specimens and labels to a uniform height on the pin.

DOUBLE MOUNTS

Small insects which cannot be pinned directly through the body with regular insect pins should be mounted on card points or on "minuten nadeln."

Card points are slender triangles of paper. These are pinned through the broad end with a regular insect pin (No. 2 or 3), and the specimen is glued to the point, as illustrated in figure 11, *A*. The card points should be pinned at the height obtained by using the highest step on the pinning block (fig. 10). Card points may be cut with scissors from a strip of paper three-eighths inch wide, but a punch,

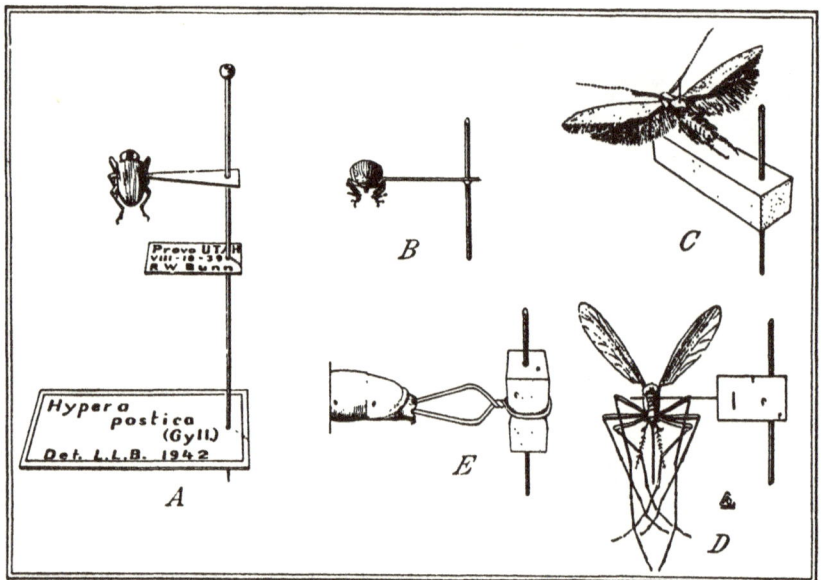

FIGURE 11.—Double mounts for small insects: *A*, Position of card point and labels on the pin; *B*, details of attachment of specimen to card point; *C*, small moth, order Lepidoptera, pinned with a "minute nadel" to a block of pith on a regular insect pin; *D*, a mosquito, order Diptera, pinned with a "minute nadel" to a block of cork on a regular insect pin; *E*, method of attaching an inflated larva to a regular insect pin by twisting fine wire around a block of cork.

obtainable from supply houses, makes better and more uniform points. A good-quality linen ledger paper should be used; "substance 36" is recommended. To fasten the specimen to the point ordinary glue may be used, but it is not recommended because it tends to become brittle. Some of the clear acetate cellulose cements, such as "Ambroid," which may be purchased in small quantities at variety stores, are satisfactory. An adequate supply may be made by dissolving a transparent resin toothbrush handle in a small amount of banana oil (amyl acetate). Pure white shellac is also fairly satisfactory but may be difficult to obtain. Whatever adhesive is used, it should not be permitted to get so thick that it "strings," and only a small amount should be used.

To mount most insects the tip of the card point should be bent down at a slight angle so that when the insect is in an upright position the bent tip of the point fits against the side of the insect (fig. 11, *B*). Only a very small part of the point should be bent; a little practice will make it easy to judge how much of the point should be bent and at what angle to fit the particular specimen that is being mounted. Most insects that are mounted on points should be attached to the point by the *right* side, although there are a few exceptions to this rule. A convenient method is to arrange the insects on their backs or left sides with their heads toward the worker; then, with the pin held in the left hand, touch a bit of adhesive to the bent point and apply it to the right side of the insect. If the tip of the point can be slipped between the body of the insect and an adjacent leg, a stronger mount will result. The insect should be attached to the point by the side of the thorax, not by the wing, abdomen, or head.

Some insects, too heavy to be held on the point by the adhesive and not large enough to be pinned with regular pins, may be attached to card points by puncturing the right side at the place where the card point would normally be placed and inserting in this puncture the tip of an unbent card point with a little adhesive on it. For puncturing specimens a needle ground to make a small, sharp scalpel is best.

To conserve pins and space in the collection it is sometimes advantageous to mount two or three specimens *of the same species* on card points on a single pin. These may be arranged one below the other at different levels, or may be fanned out at the same level.

"Minuten nadeln" are very small steel pins without heads which are used to pin small insects on a piece of cork or pith, which is then pinned on a regular insect pin, as illustrated in figure 11, *C, D*.

As with direct pinning, insects mounted on double mounts should be prepared according to standard practices. For the commoner groups these are as follows:

1. Beetles, bugs, leafhoppers, etc.: Mount on card points with the tip bent down and attached to the *right* side of the specimen (fig. 11, *A, B*).

2. Small parasitic wasps: Mount on unbent card points with the adhesive applied to the *left* side of the specimen and the feet toward the pin.

3. Small moths: Mount on "minuten nadeln" thrust through the middle of the thorax from above and with the abdomen of the specimen toward the insect pin (fig. 11, *C*).

4. Small flies and mosquitoes: Pin with "minuten nadeln" through the *side* of the thorax with the *right* side of the specimen toward the insect pin (fig. 11, *D*). Some workers prefer small flies fastened directly to regular insect pins by a bit of adhesive applied to the right side of the specimen.

INFLATION OF LARVAE

Although inflated larvae are not recommended as specimens intended for critical scientific study, it is sometimes desirable to inflate larvae for exhibition purposes. To do this the following simple equipment is needed:

1. A piece of finely drawn glass tubing furnished with clips held in place by a small rubber band (fig. 12).

2. A tin can or box to serve as an oven, and a spirit lamp or some other heating unit.

Place the larva on a clean blotter and force the body contents out by gently rolling a piece of glass tubing or round pencil from just back of the head to the end of the abdomen, being careful not to break off spines and hairs. Insert the drawn end of the glass tubing into the anal opening of the larva and secure it in place with the clips. Blow gently into the glass tubing so that the larva is distended to its normal size but not distorted, and bake it in the oven until dry, blowing the specimen meanwhile so it does not collapse, and being careful not to scorch it. When it is thoroughly dry, carefully remove it from the glass tubing by means of a fine dissecting needle and mount it on a twisted wire as shown in figure 11, *E*. This kind of mounting is quite firm if the twisted wire extends inside the larva for about two-thirds the length of the specimen.

FIGURE 12.—Tip of drawn glass tubing, showing clips holding larva in place for inflation.

RIKER MOUNTS

Occasionally it is desirable to arrange specimens for exhibition in such a way that they may be freely handled without injury. This may be done in various ways, but the method most frequently employed is to use the so-called Riker mount. This consists of a flat cardboard box filled with cotton on which the unpinned specimens are placed and covered with a glass top which holds them in place. Riker mounts may be purchased from most supply houses.

SPREADING BOARDS AND BLOCKS

The construction and use of the spreading board are illustrated in figure 13. The active collector will find it advantageous to have several boards with the middle grooves of different widths to accommodate insects of various sizes, but for general purposes a board made from the following materials will be satisfactory:

1. A hardwood base, ¼ by 4 by 12 inches.
2. Two hardwood endpieces, ½ by ¾ by 4 inches.
3. Two softwood toppieces, ⅜ by 1⅞ by 12 inches.
4. One flat strip of cork, ¼ by 1 by 11 inches.

When assembled as illustrated, the softwood toppieces leave a groove one-quarter inch wide. On the underside of these the cork strip is glued so that it covers the space between the toppieces.

Specimens must be thoroughly relaxed for spreading; otherwise they will be broken. Figure 13 shows the wings on the left side of the specimen spread in the proper manner. The first step in spreading the wings, after pinning the specimen in the groove at the proper height, is shown on the right side of the board in figure 13. To com-

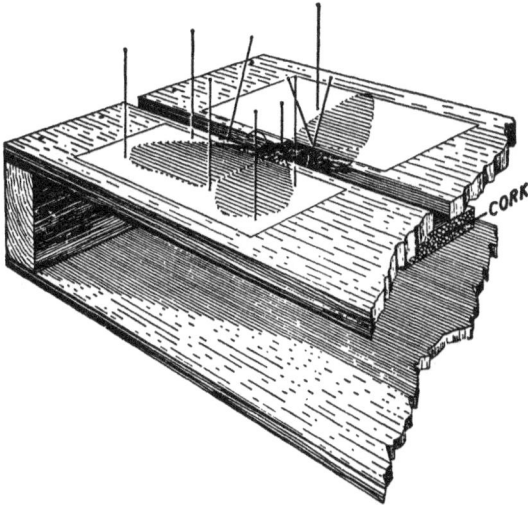

FIGURE 13.—Portion of a spreading board, showing construction of the board and steps in the process of spreading the wings and arranging the abdomen and antennae of a butterfly, order Lepidoptera.

plete the process, hold the strip of semitransparent paper covering the wings gently with the fingers of one hand and pull the wings forward with an insect pin until the hind margin of the forewing is at right angles to the body of the insect. The hind wing should then be brought forward until its front margin is just under the hind margin of the forewing. Pin both wings in place with plenty of pins arranged around them, not through them. The abdomen and antennae should also be held in place by pins. The paper strips holding the wings in place should be of fairly thin, not stiff, paper.

The spreading block is a modification of the spreading board, designed to accommodate very small moths and other small insects. Its construction and use are illustrated in figure 14. The top of the block

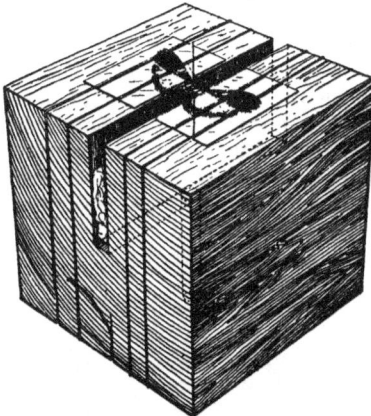

FIGURE 14.—Construction and use of the spreading block for small insects.

should be flat and smooth; the groove may be of any desired width. A hole should be drilled through the center of the block to permit the insect pin or "minute nadel" to extend below the level of the groove, and the bottom of the groove should be packed with cellu-cotton or fitted with a strip of soft pith. When insects are mounted on the spreading block, thin, flat, rectangular pieces of celluloid are used to hold the wings in place. After the wings are properly arranged, each side of the block should be wrapped, but not too tightly, with a piece of thread, as illustrated. The spreading of very small insects is a task requiring considerable skill and patience.

Specimens should be left on the spreading board or block until thoroughly dry. For large insects this requires 2 or 3 weeks; smaller specimens will dry in less time. During this time they should be stored in pestproof containers. Do not forget the collection-data label, which should be asociated with the specimen at all times.

RELAXING JARS

Insects that have dried after being killed in the cyanide bottle must be relaxed before they are mounted. This can easily be done in a relaxing jar made as follows: Into a wide-mouth jar or can with a tight cover put an inch or two of clean sand; saturate the sand with water to which a few drops of phenol (carbolic acid) have been added to keep mold from growing; cover the sand with a piece or two of cardboard cut to fit the jar, and it is ready for use. Specimens must not come in direct contact with the water and should not be left in the relaxer too long or they will be spoiled. From 1 to 3 days is usually sufficient. A relaxer should not be left where it will get too warm, or it will "sweat" on the inside.

LABELING THE SPECIMENS

During the course of preparation and mounting, specimens should have associated with them a temporary label giving essential information as to date and place of collection; and before they are put away in the collection they should be labeled with a permanent label, which is either pinned below the specimen if the specimen is mounted, or is placed in the vial if the specimen is preserved in liquid. These labels are usually small, and for that reason the data that can be given must be restricted to the most important information. Any additional information about the specimen or specimens should be kept in field notes, which can be associated with the proper material by means of lot numbers or some other convenient system. When specimens are sent for identification they should always be accompanied by all available information.

WHAT INFORMATION IS ESSENTIAL

The following information should be given on the label or labels for each specimen:

1. Locality: The place of collection should be given as exactly as possible and should be so designated that it can be found on a good map. If the place of collection does not appear on a map, it may be given in terms of the approximate direction and distance from some landmark or town.

2. Date: The day, month, and year should be given.

3. Collector: The collector should be indicated as a possible source of further information omitted from the label.

4. Source: If known, the host, food plant, or material attacked should be indicated.

If a system of lot numbers is used to associate specimens with field notes, of course the lot number should appear on the label also. A convenient method of filing field notes without the necessity of using lot numbers is to arrange them according to year, month, and day, so that the date on the label also serves as a key to the notes.

Properly prepared field notes enable the careful observer to retain much detailed information that cannot be included on the labels attached to the specimens. The type of information needed usually involves further details as to locality, the general ecological aspects of the area, the exact conditions under which the insect was found, its abundance, its behavior, how it looks in life, and so on.

HOW TO MAKE LABELS

Labels should be on good-quality paper, heavy enough so that it will stay flat when the labels are cut out, of a texture so that it will not come loose on the pin, and with a surface that can be written on with a fine pen; linen ledger paper, "substance 36," is recommended. The ink should be permanent and should not "run" if the labels are placed in jars containing liquid preservative.

Labels may be lettered by hand or printed with small type. The latter method is much better from every standpoint and is usually advisable if more than a few labels of a kind are needed. Complete or partially printed labels may be purchased from supply houses. Some sample arrangements for pin labels are shown in figure 15. To conserve space on small labels, it is well to omit punctuation and to abbreviate long locality names whenever possible.

The size of the pin labels will depend somewhat upon the insects for which they are intended. Very small labels, necessary for small specimens mounted on points, are not suitable for large moths, butterflies, cicadas, etc., because they cannot be easily read when pinned

FIGURE 15.—Sample strips of pin labels, some complete and some with the date omitted, so that by writing in the date with a fine pen a single lot of labels will serve for many different days of collecting in the same locality.

below these large-bodied insects. On the other hand, large labels, suitable for the larger insects, take up too much room in the collection if used for small specimens. Labels printed with 4-point type or diamond type will be found suitable for most purposes. Labels may also be made any size by printing a few of them in strips in large type, having an etching made at the desired reduction, and printing the desired number of labels from the etching. The labels in figure 15 were made in that way.

HOW LABELS SHOULD BE PINNED

In general, labels should be attached so that they are balanced with the mounted specimen. Figure 11, *A*, illustrates how to pin labels for specimens mounted on points; for pinned specimens the long axis of the label should coincide with the long axis of the specimen, and the left margin of the label should be toward the head of the specimen. The label may be run up on the pin to the desired height by using the pinning block; the middle step will usually give about the right height.

CARE OF THE COLLECTION

HOUSING

The adoption of standard equipment for housing the collection is advantageous, as it assures uniformity of containers when additions are necessary. Standard equipment is obtainable from any of several reliable supply houses.

Material preserved in liquid need receive no attention other than replacement of preservative and corks. Vials should be examined periodically to be sure the specimens do not become dry. Small vials may be stored in racks in such a way that the corks are not in constant contact with the liquid; this also expedites arrangement and examination of the material. Vials that cannot be inspected frequently should have the corks replaced with cotton plugs and be placed upside down in a jar large enough to hold several vials, and the jar partially filled with the preservative.

Pinned specimens should be housed in pestproof boxes. Standard insect boxes, called Schmitt boxes, are recommended. If other boxes, such as cork-lined cigar boxes, are used, they must be examined frequently for evidence of pest damage and fumigated periodically. Even pestproof boxes should be fumigated occasionally, lest a pest gain entrance and damage all the specimens. Most entomological institutions store their collections in glass-top drawers fitted with cork-lined trays of various sizes which can be shifted and arranged without the necessity of repinning specimens.

PROTECTION FROM PESTS

A few simple precautions against museum pests, such as carpet beetles, are a necessary part of the care of material not preserved in liquid. Naphthalene, which may be obtained as ordinary moth balls or in flake form, is inexpensive and satisfactory as a repellent, but it will not kill pests once they have gained access to the collection.

To kill pests it is necessary to use some fumigant such as paradichlorobenzene (PDB), carbon disulfide, ethylene dichloride, or carbon tetrachloride. Any of these may be obtained from a druggist; the first is a white crystalline substance, the others are liquids. Carbon disulfide is probably the most widely used and is very effective, but has the disadvantages of being inflammable and explosive when mixed with air in certain proportions, and having an unpleasant odor; furthermore, it will stain insect boxes.

A small amount of naphthalene or paradichlorobenzene may be included in each box of specimens, either in a cloth bag or a small box with a perforated top firmly pinned in the corner. Naphthalene in the form of moth balls may be pinned in the box by attaching the ball to an ordinary pin. To do this, heat the head of the pin, force it into the moth ball, and permit it to cool.

Liquid fumigants may be used without the danger of staining the boxes by saturating a cotton plug and placing it in a short, widemouthed vial pinned in the corner.

All moth balls or fumigant containers should be removed from boxes before they are shipped.

PACKING AND SHIPPING SPECIMENS

LIVE INSECTS

Adult insects intended for a collection or submitted for identification should not be shipped alive. The shipment of live insects is controlled by Federal law; permits to ship certain insects alive may be obtained from the Bureau of Entomology and Plant Quarantine, Washington 25, D. C.

Pupae or larvae sent for rearing should be enclosed in tight containers, such as tin salve boxes or mailing cases, depending upon the size and number of specimens. Pupae preferably should be packed loosely in moist (but not wet) moss. Larvae should be packed with sufficient food material to last until their arrival at their destination. Most beetle larvae and some moth larvae, especially cutworms, should be isolated, since they are more or less cannibalistic. To prevent excess accumulation of frass and sweating, do not overload the container with specimens or plant material. Do not put ventholes in the containers; insects require a minimum of air and will not suffocate.

Live Hemiptera and other small active insects may be shipped in mailing cases with a few stems of their host plant (with the leaves removed) set in paraffin. Insects such as these are easily killed by excess moisture in the container, and for this reason a number of tiny ventholes are advisable.

Bulky insects, or pieces of host plants bearing insects such as scale insects, should be partially or completely dried before being placed in a container, or should be packed in a container which will permit drying to continue after closure; otherwise they will decay and be worthless.

DEAD INSECTS

Mounted insects should be firmly pinned in a box securely lined with cork or some other suitable material. If the specimen is heavy, or if the pin carries some other heavy object such as a small vial, additional pins should be set firmly on each side of the specimen or vial to prevent them from rotating on the pin and to keep the pin from coming out of the cork. Heavy specimens or objects loose in a box can break all the other specimens in the container.

PACKING FOR SHIPMENT

Vials should be wrapped separately in strong paper and then packed in a mailing case or strong box with cotton or cellucotton around them so they cannot shift about. Vials containing any except very small specimens should be full of liquid or have a tight plug of cotton inserted at the surface of the liquid so that the specimens cannot splash about. Be sure that the cork fits and is firmly set.

Pill boxes should be packed snugly in a stout container with some packing around them. Boxes of mounted specimens, as well as most other containers, should be placed in a larger carton with at least 2 inches of excelsior, straw, or crumpled paper packed tightly enough all around to hold the container in place, yet loosely enough to be resilient.

Do not put loose naphthalene or paradichlorobenzene in either pill boxes or insect boxes that are being shipped. Never send insects in ordinary envelopes; they are invariably crushed and worthless.

Always send as complete information as possible with specimens submitted for identification. Labels carrying data should be so attached or enclosed that there is no doubt as to which specimens they belong with.

RECOGNITION OF MATERIAL

Because of the enormous number of insect species, anything even approximating a complete classification is impossible in this bulletin. The following brief section on identification is designed to aid the collector in recognizing the commoner and more important general groups with sufficient accuracy to follow the instructions previously given.

Insects are classified as belonging to orders, and all insects of the same general kind belong to the same order. For example, all moths and butterflies are included in the order Lepidoptera, all beetles belong to the order Coleoptera, and so on. These orders are divided into families, the families are further divided into genera (singular, genus), and each genus may include from one to many species. A species is a particular kind, as distinguished from the more or less general kinds of insects that make up the genera, families, and orders. Each known species of insect has a scientific name, which consists of the generic name, the specific (species) name, and the name of the man who described and named the insect. For example, *Musca domestica* Linnaeus is the scientific name of the common housefly; *Musca*

FIGURE 16.—Thysanura. The firebrat (*Thermobia domestica Pack.*), a bristletail common in houses. Actual length without the tails and antennae about 8 mm.

is the generic name, *domestica* is the specific name, and the fly was first named by Linnaeus.

Synopses of the major orders of insects are given in the sections that follow. For more detailed information on classification, one or more books such as those following should be consulted:

COLLEGE ENTOMOLOGY. E. O. ESSIG. 900 pp., illus. 1942. New York.

FIELD BOOK OF INSECTS. F. E. LUTZ. 509 pp., illus. 1918. New York.

HOW TO KNOW THE INSECTS. H. E. JAQUES. Iowa Acad. Sci. Biol. Survey Pub. 1, 140 pp., illus. 1936. St. Louis, Chicago [etc.].

AN INTRODUCTION TO ENTOMOLOGY. J. H. COMSTOCK. 234 pp., illus. 1888. Ithaca, N. Y. (Completely rewritten 1920.)

THYSANURA

Thysanura (silverfish, bristletails) are wingless insects with long antennae and usually with three long taillike appendages. The mouth parts are formed for chewing. The young resemble the adults. (See fig. 16.) They are usually found in moist situations around houses or out of doors under stones and boards. They are flat and can run rapidly and hide in cracks and crevices. Occasionally they do some damage to bookbindings and curtains.

COLLEMBOLA

Collembola (springtails) are tiny wingless insects which jump by means of a taillike appendage that folds under the body. The mouth parts are formed for chewing. The young resemble the adults. Springtails are common in moist situations and in leafmold. Some species are important pests in greenhouses and mushroom cellars.

ORTHOPTERA AND DERMAPTERA

Orthoptera (grasshoppers, crickets, katydids, roaches, mantids, and walkingsticks), and dermaptera (earwigs) generally have two pairs of wings which have many veins; the front pair are usually slender and

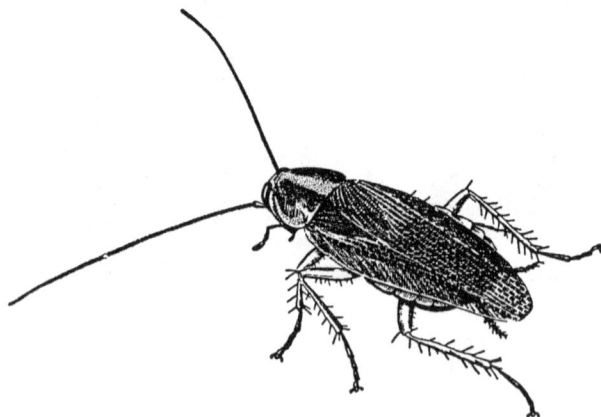

FIGURE 17.—Orthoptera. German cockroach (*Blattella germanica* (L.)), the common cockroach usually found in houses in cities. Actual length about 16 mm.

the hind pair broad and fanlike. The mouth parts are formed for chewing. The nymphs resemble the adults. Grasshoppers are well known for the damage they do to crops, and cockroaches are among our commonest household pests. (See fig. 17.)

ISOPTERA

Isoptera (termites, or "white ants") are small, soft-bodied insects The workers are wingless. The reproductive forms have two pairs of large wings with many veins. The mouth parts are formed for chewing. The workers are found in colonies in wood in contact with the ground. The reproductive winged forms (fig. 18) are frequently seen swarming on warm days. These insects are frequently called "white ants," but they are not true ants and may be distinguished from ants by the fact that the abdomen is broadly attached to the thorax. Some species are very destructive to buildings, especially in warm or tropical regions.

FIGURE 18.—Isoptera. The winged form of *Reticulitermes flavipes* (Koll.), a common and destructive termite. Actual length about 10 mm. The wingless workers are smaller and dull white in color.

PLECOPTERA

Plecoptera (stoneflies) are rather large, soft-bodied insects with long legs and antennae, two pairs of large wings with not many veins, and two long, taillike appendages. The mouth parts are formed for chewing but are usually vestigial in the adults. The young, or nymphal stages, live in streams, and the adults are found near streams. (See fig. 19.)

FIGURE 19.—Plecoptera. *Neoperla clymene* (Newm.), a stonefly common east of the Rocky Mountains. Actual length about 14 mm.

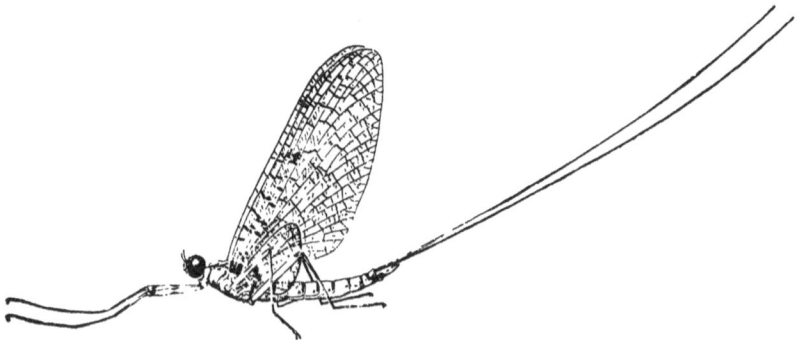

FIGURE 20.—Ephemeroptera. *Stenonema canadense* (Walk.), a common Mayfly. Actual length of body about 9 mm.

EPHEMEROPTERA

Ephemeroptera (Mayflies) are delicate insects with two pairs of triangular-shaped wings with many veins, the front pair large, the hind pair small. They have long front legs and two or three very long, taillike appendages. The mouth parts of the adults are vestigial; those of the immature stages are fitted for chewing. (See fig. 20.) The immature stages are aquatic and do not resemble the adults. The adults are common around water, especially in spring, when they often emerge in enormous numbers. They are an important fish food.

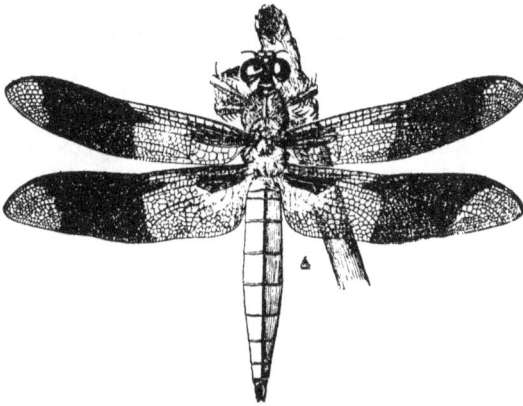

FIGURE 21.—Odonata. *Plathemis lydia* (Drury), a dragonfly. Actual length about 45 mm.

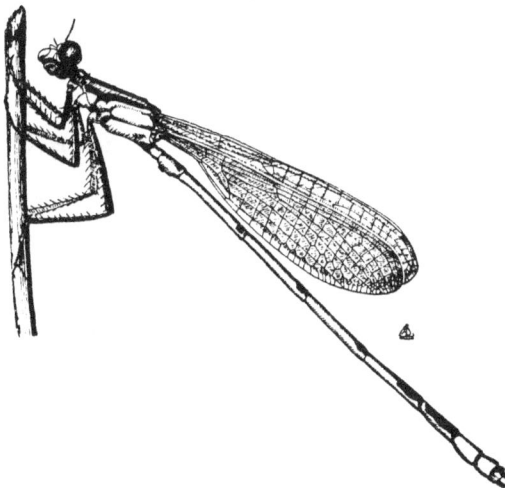

FIGURE 22.—Odonata. *Enallagma exsulans* Hagen, a damselfly. Actual length about 40 mm.

ODONATA

Odonata (dragonflies, damselflies) are large insects with two pairs of membranous, many-veined wings, the hind pair as large as or larger than the front pair. The mouth parts are formed for chewing. The immature stages are aquatic and unlike the adults. They are common around ponds, lakes, and streams. Both the adults and the immature stages feed on other insects, and because they feed at least to some extent on mosquitoes and other small flies they are beneficial.

CORRODENTIA

Corrodentia (psocids or booklice) are small, either winged or wingless; the winged members have two pairs of wings with a few, mostly crooked, veins. The antennae are long; the mouth parts are formed for chewing. The immature stages resemble the adults. These insects are common around old paper and books and are found out of doors on trunks and leaves of trees, or on stones or other places where lichens and fungi grow. They are gregarious and feed upon lichens and vegetable matter. Some of the species are annoying household pests. (See fig. 23.)

FIGURE 23.—Corrodentia. The booklouse (*Liposcelis divinitorius* (Müll.)), a common species. Actual length about 1 mm.

MALLOPHAGA

Mallophaga (biting lice or bird lice) are small, flat, wingless, parasitic insects with mouth parts formed for chewing. The legs and antennae are short. The immature stages resemble the adults. These insects feed upon feathers of birds or on hair and skin scales of other animals. They are frequently important pests of domestic fowls and animals.

ANOPLURA

Anoplura (true lice or sucking lice) are small, flat, wingless, parasitic insects with mouth parts formed for piercing and sucking. The legs and antennae are short. The immature stages resemble the adults.

These insects are commonly found on domestic animals but not on fowls. The human louse, or "cootie," belongs to this order. They feed by sucking blood and are frequently important pests of domestic animals and man. The common cootie, or body louse of man, transmits the dread typhus fever, a disease which may become especially serious in time of war.

THYSANOPTERA

Thysanoptera (thrips) are mostly very small insects, usually with two pairs of slender wings with few veins but fringed with long hairs; the legs and antennae are short. The mouth parts are formed for piercing and sucking, and the immature stages resemble the adults. (See fig. 24.) Some of these insects feed on plants; others are predaceous on small insects. Those that feed on plants are frequently very injurious in greenhouses or on truck crops.

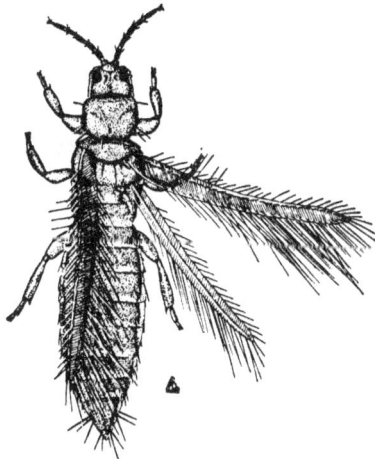

FIGURE 24.—Thysanoptera. The flower thrips (*Frankliniella tritici* (Fitch)), a common species. Actual length about 1 mm.

HEMIPTERA

Hemiptera (true bugs, cicadas, leafhoppers, aphids, scale insects, and their allies) are either winged or wingless, the winged members having two pairs of wings, the front pair frequently somewhat thickened, the hind pair membranous. The mouth parts are formed for piercing and sucking. The immature stages resemble the adults. (See figs. 25, 26, 27, and 28.) Most members of this order feed on plant juices, but some are predaceous on other insects, and some, such as the bedbug, suck blood from animals or man. Most forms are terrestrial, but some are aquatic. The plant-feeding forms include some species like the chinch bug and some scale insects that cause a great deal of damage to crops; other species are known to transmit virus diseases of plants.

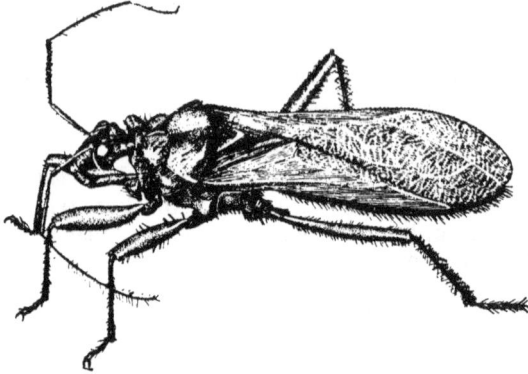

FIGURE 25.—Hemiptera. The masked hunter (*Reduvius personatus* (L.)), a true bug. Actual length about 18 mm.

FIGURE 26.—Hemiptera. *Draeculacephala minerva* Ball, a leafhopper. Actual length about 9 mm.

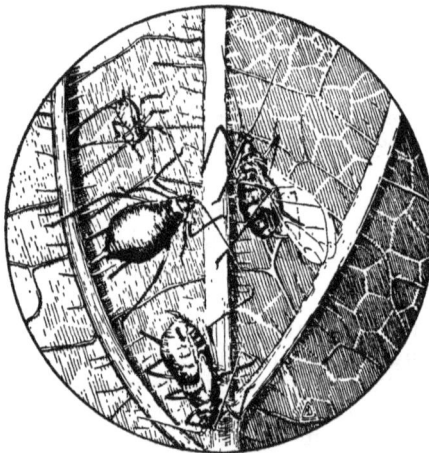

FIGURE 27.—Hemiptera. Aphids, *Macrosiphum ambrosiae* (Thomas), on a leaf of giant ragweed, winged and wingless forms and young. Actual length of body of adult about 1.7 mm.

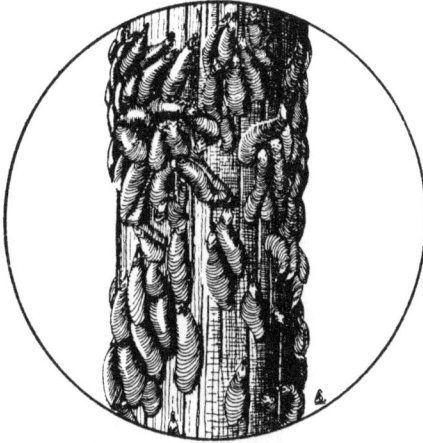

FIGURE 28.—Hemiptera. The oystershell scale (*Lepidosaphes ulmi* (L.)), on lilac. Actual length of the large scale insects about 2.5 mm.

COLEOPTERA

Coleoptera (beetles and weevils) are usually winged, with two pairs of wings, the front pair thick and forming a hard shell and meeting in a straight line down the middle of the back. The hind wings are membranous and are folded under the front wings when at rest. The mouth parts are formed for chewing. The immature stages are grub-like or wormlike, and the insects pass through a pupal stage before becoming adults. The food habits are varied; some feed on living plants, some are predaceous, some are scavengers, and some bore in wood. This order includes some of the best known and most important of our insect enemies. (See figs. 29, 30, 31, and 32.) Most of the members are terrestrial but a few are aquatic.

FIGURE 29.—Coleoptera. Striped blister beetle (*Epicauta vittata* (F.)). Actual length about 18 mm.

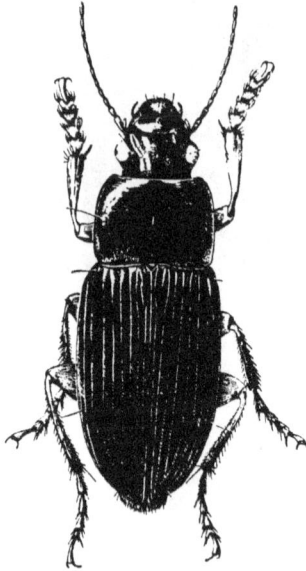

FIGURE 30.—Coleoptera. *Harpalus pennsylvanicus* Deg., a ground beetle. Actual length about 16 mm.

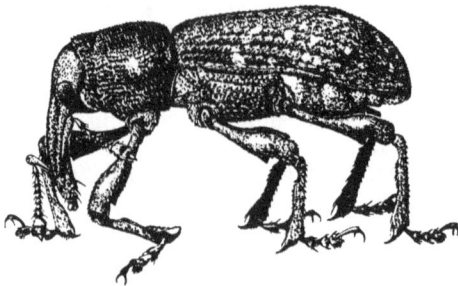

FIGURE 31.—Coleoptera. Pales weevil (*Hylobius pales* (Hbst.)). Actual length about 10 mm.

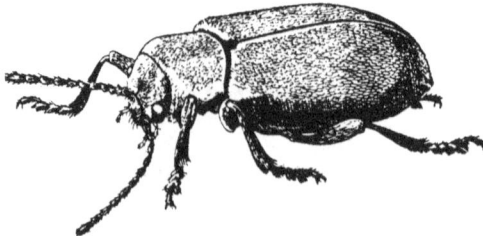

FIGURE 32.—Coleoptera. *Glyptoscelis squamulata* Crotch, a leaf beetle. Actual length about 9.5 mm.

NEUROPTERA

Neuroptera (lacewing flies, ant lions, and their allies) are rather fragile insects with two pairs of many-veined wings of about the same size; the antennae are long. (See fig. 33.) The mouth parts are formed for chewing. The immature stages are predaceous. The commonest ones are the aphid lion, and the "doodle-bug," or ant lion, which forms pits in dry, dusty places. Because they feed on insect pests they are beneficial.

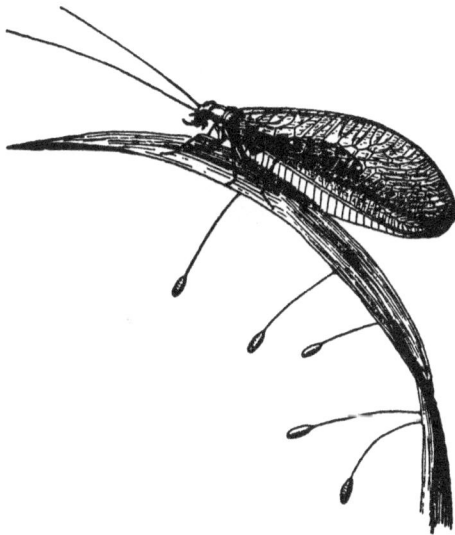

FIGURE 33.—Neuroptera. *Chrysopa oculata* Say, a common green lacewing fly, and eggs attached to plant. Actual length of adult about 13 mm.

ZORAPTERA

Zoraptera are small insects, either winged or wingless, the winged members with two pairs of wings with few veins. The antennae are rather long. The mouth parts are formed for chewing. The immature stages resemble the adults. These little-known insects live under bark of trees and under boards and slabs of wood on old sawdust piles. They somewhat resemble termites and might easily be mistaken for them but are considerably smaller.

MEGALOPTERA

Megaloptera (alder flies, dobson flies) are rather large insects with two pairs of similar wings with many veins. The antennae are long. The mouth parts are formed for chewing. The immature stages, which are aquatic, are unlike the adults. (See fig. 34.) The immature stage of the dobson fly is the hellgrammite, familiar to fishermen and much prized as bait. The adults are found near streams.

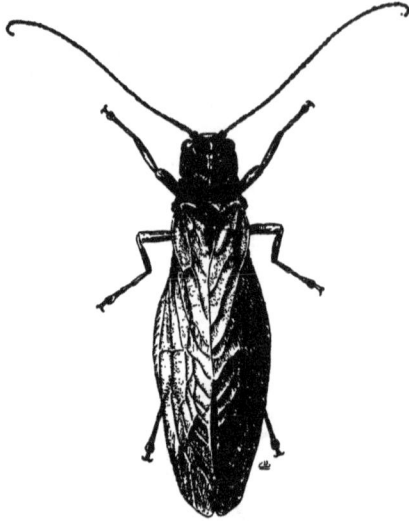

FIGURE 34.—Megaloptera. *Sialis infumata* Newm., an alder fly. Actual length about 13 mm.

MECOPTERA

Mecoptera (scorpion flies and their allies) are usually winged, the winged members having two pairs of similar wings which are usually rather long and narrow and have several veins. The legs and antennae are long. (See fig. 35.) The mouth parts are formed for chewing. Immature stages are somewhat like caterpillars. These insects are found in moist, shaded woods. The adults are predaceous. The immature stages live in soil litter.

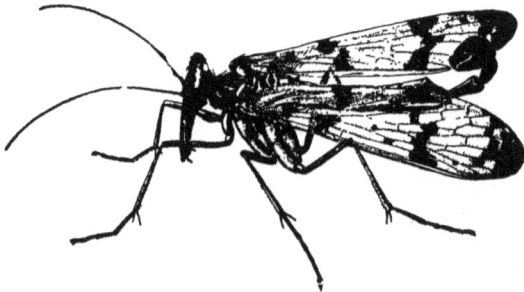

FIGURE 35.—Mecoptera. *Panorpa rufescens* Ramb., a scorpion fly. Actual length about 12 mm.

TRICHOPTERA

Trichoptera (caddisflies) are soft-bodied insects with two pairs of wings clothed with silky hairs and having a medium number of veins. The antennae are long. The mouth parts of the adults are vestigial.

The immature stages are wormlike and live in water. Most of them build cases about their bodies. The adults are common around streams. (See fig. 36.)

FIGURE 36.—Trichoptera. *Phryganea vestita* (Walk.), a caddisfly. Actual length about 20 mm.

LEPIDOPTERA

Lepidoptera (butterflies, moths) are usually winged, the winged members having two pairs of wings covered with overlapping scales. (See fig. 37.) The mouth parts of the adults are formed for sucking. The immature stages are wormlike and are known as caterpillars, cutworms, or hornworms. Their mouth parts are formed for chewing. This is one of the best known orders of insects and contains some of our most important pests, such as the codling moth, the armyworm, clothes moths, cabbage worms, and many other common forms. Most of the species feed on leaves of plants in the immature stages, but others bore in plant stems and some are leaf miners.

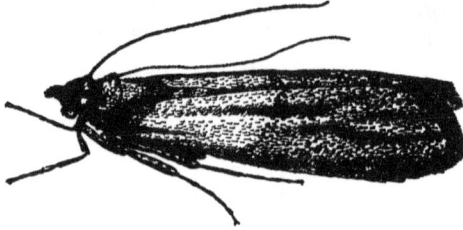

FIGURE 37.—Lepidoptera. The Indian-meal moth (*Plodia interpunctella* (Hbn.)),
a common pest of stored grain. Actual length about 11 mm.

DIPTERA

Diptera (flies, mosquitoes, gnats, and their allies) are usually
winged, but have only one pair of wings with not many veins; the
hind wings are represented by a pair of slender, knobbed structures
called halteres. The mouth parts are formed for sucking or piercing
and sucking. (See figs. 38 and 39.) The immature stages are wormlike and are usually known as maggots; they are entirely unlike the
adults. The order includes forms that are parasitic, others that are
predaceous, and others that live on either living or dead plant material.
Because many of the species carry diseases, this is one of the most
important orders from the standpoint of human welfare. Other members of the order cause a great amount of damage to crops.

FIGURE 38.—Diptera. *Sarcophaga haemorroidalis* (Fall.), a flesh fly. Actual
length about 15 mm.

FIGURE 39.—Diptera. The striped horsefly (*Tabanus lineola* (F.)). Actual length about 15 mm.

SIPHONAPTERA

Siphonaptera (fleas) are small, wingless insects with the body laterally compressed; the legs are comparatively long; the body has numerous short bristles directed backward. The mouth parts are formed for piercing and sucking. The immature stages are wormlike, quite different from the adults, and are found in the nests of various animals. The adults are well known as pests of domestic animals and man; one species transmits bubonic plague, an important disease in tropical countries.

FIGURE 40.—Hymenoptera. The introduced pine sawfly (*Diprion simile* (Htg.)). Male at left; female at right. Actual length about 10 mm.

HYMENOPTERA

Hymenoptera (bees, wasps, ants, and their allies) are winged or wingless insects, the winged members with two pairs of membranous wings with few veins. The mouth parts are formed for chewing or for both chewing and sucking. The immature stages are maggotlike or caterpillarlike and entirely different from the adults. The habits of these insects are varied; some are predaceous, some are parasitic, some cause plant galls, some feed on plant foliage, and some, such as bumblebees and honeybees, live on plant pollen and nectar. This order includes some of our most harmful and some of our most beneficial insects. (See figs. 40, 41, and 42.)

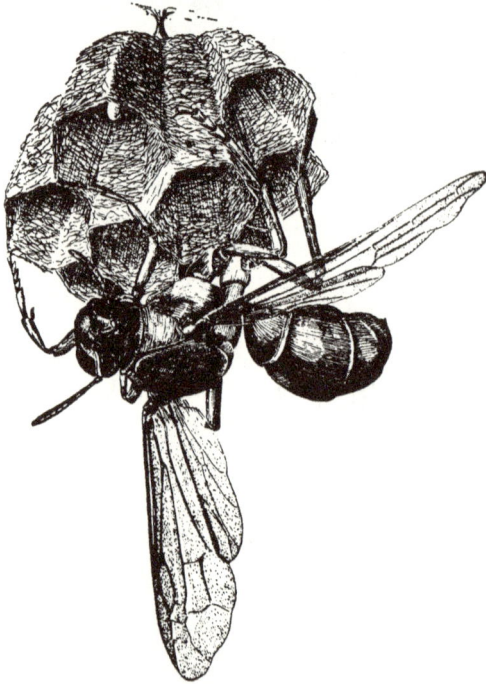

FIGURE 41.—Hymenoptera. *Polistes fuscatus* var. *pallipes* Lep., a wasp that makes a paper nest. Actual length about 20 mm.

FIGURE 42.—Hymenoptera. *Camponotus castaneus* (Latr.), a common ant. Actual length about 9 mm.